CLOUDBURST and CONSTELLATIONS

© Lou Smith   2025

The author acknowledges the traditional owners of the land and waterways where she lives and works, the Wurundjeri Woi-wurrong people of the Kulin Nation. This book was written on the unceded lands of the Wurundjeri Woi-wurrong, Awabakal and Worimi peoples. The author pays her respects to their Elders past, present and future.

All rights reserved. Except for appropriate use in a book review, no part of this publication may be reproduced, stored in a retrieval system, or transmitted in any form or by any means, without the prior permission of the publisher, or in the case of photocopying or reprographic copying, a licence from the Copyright Agency of Australia.

Cloudburst and Constellations

ISBN 9781763825956

Front cover artwork *Spiderweb* | Kyoko Imazu

Author photograph | Josie Newton

Walleah Press
South Launceston
Tasmania, Australia 7249

www.walleahpress.com.au
ralph-walleahpress@proton.me

Cloudburst and Constellations

Lou Smith

Lou Smith is a poet and researcher of Welsh, Jamaican and English heritage who grew up in Muloobinba/Newcastle, NSW and now lives and works in Narrm/Melbourne, Victoria. She has a PhD in Creative Writing from the University of Melbourne. Lou has been the recipient of a Wheeler Centre Hot Desk Fellowship, a Lighthouse Arts at Nobbys-Whibayganba Headland residency and the Gunyah Artist-in-Residence programme. Her poetry and critical essays have been published in journals and anthologies such as *Australian Poetry Journal*, *Liberation Begins in the Imagination: Writings on Caribbean-British Art*, *Rabbit*, *Cordite*, *Wasafiri*, *Journal of Women's History*, *The Caribbean Writer* and *Mascara Literary Review*. Lou is the author of *riversalt* (Flying Island Books).

Contents

Cloudburst	1
calidris ruficollis (smallest shorebird in Australia), a migration	4
Light	5
After the downpour	6
Cataract	7
When the Rain Came	8
'White Spill'	9
Fault Lines	10
Mapping	11
Weep	12
Evidence of Life	13
Held	14
Winter	15
Parable	16
lulling	17
(Corporeality of) Tear Sipping	18
Flor de Muertos	19
tagetes lemmonii	20
Libations (Evergreen Plantation, Louisiana)	21
The Collector	23
some other strange fish	24
(S)kin	25
Belgrave Rd	26
And I Wandered	28
On Walking to See the Exhibition *London, Sugar & Slavery*	29
Drift Seeds	30
Snowdonia National Park	32
Drought	33

Long Mountain House (College Common)	34
Drifting	35
Metamorphosis	36
Dermis	37
She is there	38
Stockton	39
Eulogy	41
Wayfinding	42
Oval	43
Home for Leaf-Curling Spiders	45
a history of nature and buildings	46
brisk	47
Heliotropism	48
sea urchin	49
Christmas Day (Sunset)	50
Ma in the Moon	51
New Year's Eve 2009	52
William and Tom	53
Home	54
Bones	55
leafless branches swinging as though breaking	56
Notes	57
Acknowledgements	59

Cloudburst

*It's been raining
for awhile now*

–Kimya Dawson

I

There is

    the before   and

        after

the present   a lingering mass
inching back in
on itself
like a jellyfish washed upon the shore

before death
this was all there is
now we cling to photos
of his cheeky grin
pale hands of
ginger-freckled skin

II

the future is inaudible

a place of no footprints

like stepping on the shoreline of a salt lake

III

the night he died
a storm blew up
and gum leaves shook like pom-poms in the wind

it rained for weeks then

we're travelling now
across country
to where the earth looks like fire
and clouds conjure the ocean
and all things metaphysical
guiding us
is a bright blue and yellow plastic boat
we don't know where he got it
(somewhere second-hand)
but it sits wedged on the curved, black dashboard
as though on a rolling sea
pointing to mother-of-pearl clouds
and those cursing under their breath

it was the flood that stopped us from crossing
the highway at Sandy Creek
so we camped on the side of the road
in a constant cloud of mosquitoes so aggressive
their bites could be mistaken for chickenpox
in the morning
his brother swam in the pool of water on the roadside
his body floating
like a snow angel
above the asphalt

calidris ruficollis (smallest shorebird in Australia), a migration

saltworks, sewage farms, saltmarsh, shallow wetlands, swamps, soaks, sandy shores, sheltered inlets, saltflats, riverbanks, lakes, waterholes, bore drains, pools, dams, flooded paddocks, damp grasslands, bays, lagoons, estuaries, coraline shores

Red-neck or Little Sandpiper, Roufus-necked Stint, Little Stint, Eastern Little Stint, Least Sandpiper, Land Snipe

nesting in the Siberian tundra and northern and western Alaska, in summer southern migration begins, stopping on the muddy shores of the Yellow Sea, crossing Australia's vast interior–pale wing stripe in flight–reaching the shores of the southern coastline –
(as light as a box of matches)

brown, grey-brown, feathers pale-edged, some black, some white

from wetlands of Wilson Inlet, crossing Australia's vast interior, refuelling on the muddy shores of the Yellow Sea, moist moss-lichen tundra to breed –

when breeding, head and nape is deep salmon-pink suffusing into the mantle and wing-coverts pink

Light

Under a flicker of stars
gold, silver and blue
the breath of those sleeping fills the night

the reflection of the full moon
forms another white boardwalk on the sea.

From the Obelisk, The Baths hide
on the edge of a model city
in the wane of amber lights

After the downpour

–warm furious raindrops–
morning imitates evening
congregating clouds of pitch and ash
melaleuca bark softened
to leathery, dusky pink
and bougainvillea, a purple
so purple it is beyond colour, escapes
over wonky, wooden fence palings
there is an internal quiet
after so much rain
streets cleansed of heat and rushing
bodies and machines
night lost to dreams
breath and sounds of sleep,
each leaf's reaching veins
seen for the first time by my baby's
wide eyes   time held
in the clarity of colours after rain

Cataract

Yesterday, we were trapped in a storm that drenched us to the bone. Lightening tore apart the sky, small fingerbones squeezed my own as we hunched and ran the best we could in rain-wet sand forty minutes back to camp. Now sea debris lies scattered along the beach. Wood and shell, mounds of seaweed tangled greens and browns like netting. And other mounds, indistinct, fleshy, mottled the palest of pinks. The beach is a graveyard of indistinguishable bodies, missing fins, and skin. We zigzag between them, in post-storm still, feet sinking

From The Skerries, comes the bellows. Moaning from atop the grey-cream rock anchored in mourning sea. Along the beach, Fur Seal pups washed up from the colony as far as the eye can see

When the Rain Came

my clothes were my second-skin
I wanted to grab hold of them and peel off
the soaked cotton that was weighing me down
peel in strips like the wet ripped sheets
Mum and Grandma used as rags
for curling my hair when I was a kid
there was no escaping
the opaque draping the city
smothering vision
liquid inhaled and ingested
footpath slick as an oil baron
in this deluge it was as if every memory
of every misdeed had risen to the surface
the spectres of London reflected
in its puddles

'White Spill'

After the floods in Queensland and Northern NSW, 2022

pontoons of polystyrene bob in wave breaks, fragmenting into tiny beads of plastic, destructive sea jewels easily mistaken for salps if only polystyrene was gelatinous. salps, however, are miraculous, swarming unnoticed and unadorned filtering the seas of carbon from surface to deep

split into chunks, the pontoons resemble barnacled rocks from some other coast where rocks look like chalk or perhaps small icebergs. so buoyant they float by in heavy seas, glacial, illusory. small pearls of polymer beans spreading

drifting like artificial food floating with wind and tide, a thing with no memory of its forming so indistinct now from its source – coal and gas and cellulose – displaced like the astroturf uprooted green upon green from the playing fields during the flooding

people used battery-powered vacuums to suck up the tiny beads in the hope that turtle hatchlings wouldn't swallow them, dolphins wouldn't ingest them, fish wouldn't eat them. polystyrene washed onto beaches amidst plastic and other debris, mushrooming across

sand, disguised in sea foam, frothing and breathing clinging to refuse and runoff, an imposter in the living sea the 'white spill', the catastrophe

Fault Lines

Off the peninsula, wide strip of cacti-covered land
bones are submerged in seabed–
Morgan and his gang,
'Calico' Jack, hanged and gibbeted on a sandbar as a warning

and in 1692 when the earth bellowed along its fault lines
people were sucked into sand
bodies spat into the sky,
ruins of buildings
forming coral cities–

now, in this golden hour
fishermen return to Port Royal
their small boats illuminated by the sun
a slither of blood orange, glorious, preceding darkness

Mapping

I was fifteen
when Grandma died.
Memory, map worn
stained by tears
dispersing salty edges.
I have no memory of Grandma's death
but I wore hot pink to her funeral
mourned with the wail of a cyhyraeth.
Still, she sits by my bed when I'm dreaming
says, 'enough of this foolishness'.
Doris, daughter of Oceanus
mother of sea-nymphs
hair roped on her head in sailor knots

Weep

After Shari Kocher's 'Not the Horses'

weep when we are lonely
weep when all is gone
weep as if this life
is a blue note in a song
the weeping branches of the willows
caressing river stones and moss
weep for I have wronged you
for life, for life's loss

Evidence of Life

After witnessing Joseph L. Griffiths' artwork *Memorial to Merlynston Creek*, as part of *Evidence of Life: MoreArt 2022*

```
mist, a spectre                                    mist, a ghost
   rising from dew                              rising from love
      covered grass                                  green grass
         for the creek                            for the creek
              now flowing through culvert
                    under Renown St
              next to the aged care centre
         where my mother           where my mother
         breathed her last         breathed her last
      breath, and memory              breath, and all
forgot itself                               came undone
```

Held

Held in leaves
sheoak's slender needles
amplifying the wail

roots wrench at river soil
slow swirl of slick eddy
sunlight a fair-weather friend

I struggle to remember
even the smallest things, and even
the smallest things are catastrophic–

the bed you once slept in, the midwife
calling me 'lovey' as you always had,
as I waited for my second child to be born

a month after you slipped away
while our heads were turned

Winter

clouds
grey as a Shrike-Thrush wing
wind
moving tree branches in exaggerated ports de bras
electricity wires, buildings
moaning an aeolian keening

Parable

More than half the sky is blood
more than half the ground is weeds
more than half the sea is plastic
more than half the world is greed

lulling

my first-born, still in the caul
his talisman, a link to the otherworld
my second, born in a flood of fluid he could have been a fish
not enough towels to mop the hospital bed

moon steals light from day
breath forms song
you sipped tiny sips of amniotic fluid
as though drinking in the body of stars

(Corporeality of) Tear Sipping

There are moths and butterflies that drink tears of turtles, elephants, cattle, crocodilians. And some that drink the tears of sleeping birds. A poetic faint flutter of wings against grief-stricken skin. Except that when thirsty some will make an animal cry by harpooning it in the eye with a barbed proboscis. For tears don't only belong to those that shed them, it seems, they nourish small, winged creatures, feed them salt, and protein. And the tears of the animals in question aren't really tears at all, perhaps, but eyes watering like a soft sun shower for growing seedlings. Perhaps we need butterflies in their brief time of sky, to quietly sip our tears, so we know our grief sustains another – wingbeat, heartbeat – so we are held as if we are home

Flor de Muertos

yellowed-brown

leaves on grape vine and mulberry tree

                                            wintering

                                                              falling

                                                                             withering

days are shorter, cooler now

                         thoughts in grey

death is all

      (encompassing)

death and the remembrance

of death

the dying– skin-yellowed, grey

tagetes lemmonii

passionfruit marigolds burst

through dying leaves

of vines

as bright as sun's serenade

sweet aroma an aubade

inviting spirits, gently listening

Libations (Evergreen Plantation, Louisiana)

Through the symmetry of the
Georgian garden's hedges,
we walked in deliberation
down the long dirt road
the long dirt road lined with oaks
swishing ash-like trails of Spanish Moss
long and silver-grey like foxes' tails.

Twelve small huts lined the road
twelve small, grey wooden huts
– huts far smaller than the pidgeonniers
where pigeons were kept for eating –
twelve small, grey huts, that once
housed fifty-four people –
two families in each.

When Eintou began the libations
camphor flaming in its bamboo vessel
droplets searing earth–
trails of moss
swept low
trails of moss
reared high
trails of moss
trembled

their ash-like
tails in the sky
as we honoured
and we remembered
the Ancestors

The Collector

Here, are remains of things –
beetles, beetles' wings,
moths cottony soft.
I find them in pockets
extract them with tweezer-like precision
with my fingertips
line them up on top of the washing machine
with the care of an entomologist.
There are live ones too–
spiders in jars
millipedes in cardboard boxes
miniature insectariums
on windowsills and tables
all with labels
and accompanying diagrams.
Each day he tells me facts,
'Did you know crickets have ears on their knees?'
Peruses his animal encyclopedia religiously
moves snails away from oncoming
foot traffic with patient alacrity
watches daddy long legs sway their long lithe legs
an adagio conducted with their shadows

some other strange fish

mud rich and thick sticks to our soles – perfect time for planting

we heave blocks of bluestone, align them into paths and dry walls in our garden. native bees make home in the spaces

half-moon sits off-duty in an egg-white-whipped sky

ride our bikes over bluestone bridges, the creek glints like flint below, search for tortoise and rakali

sediment leeched with grease and metals and too-large carp

under willows sweeping lichen, we watch night herons balance on spindly yellow legs

puffy dandelions float by like some other strange fish

(S)kin

My skin now resembles my mother's
epidermis of furrows and paths
concertinas above the breastbone
contour lines on a topographic map

From Grandma's upper arms
hung a weight of flesh between tissue-thin skin
we would swing it back and forth as children
like a pendulum

Under my baby's temple
skin as thin as gum moth wings
are traces left by periwinkles
or near-far veins

Belgrave Rd

Stucco-fronted terraces
run the length of Belgrave Rd
hotels now a mirage of white plaster facades
dissolving in the glare of midday

you lived here Mum,
at number 95
below-ground watching the shoes of passers-by
ankle-wet running for buses in the rain.
Or was your view from an attic window
of the River Thames spreading
dark grey from one bank to another
rushing with an unexpected life-force
under Tower Bridge…

sweet Thames, the city's keeper, sweating oil and tar
as barges drift with the turning tide

when we were kids
you read to us from
Old Possum's Book of Practical Cats
and we'd imagine our own cats
Sally and Sue
as Mungojerrie and Rumpelteazer
running amok through the house
but perhaps it was me and my sister
in your imaginings
knocking things over with our fighting
our fingernails pressing half-moons
into each other's skin

people unknown to us
inhabit the house we grew up in
now renovated and sub-divided
their children play
in the newly-landscaped front garden
holding earthworms'
wriggly bodies
extending and retracting
in their palms

And I wandered

through streets unknown
marking your footsteps
to the chimes of Westminster Abbey
my metronome, imagined you
cowering under your bed
in '41 when fire bombs fell

though you left
forty years ago
I swear you passed me by
walking briskly in the sun
on your way to work
rushing to catch the tube to Soho
where women on high stools
hold court in doorways
and in the '50s blue notes
held sway on the breeze

or was that you sitting across
from me on the train
as it jerked its way through the city's catacombs
where we are all witnesses

On Walking to See the Exhibition *London, Sugar & Slavery*

Cobbles blue and bruising, laneways carry history on their backs. Following the tourist walk through twisting East End streets, the imprint of feet in roads sloped and sunken. The guidebook doesn't describe the discordance, the bitterness at the back of the throat. Rats squeaking, flesh and bone and blood seeped in.

At Docklands, across from business people sipping Pino Gris, I watch cranes lifting and balancing, filling spaces, girls lying on grass in their bikinis under golden summer sun.

From West India Docks ships came and went, came and went, came and went.
Cargo of rum's sticky syrup, hulls glued with blood

Drift Seeds

        air is close, salt-heavy

I know these streets
as I know my own skin

memory layering

stories travelled like drift seeds
from Wales, Jamaica and England
of my family's paths un/known to them

        memory as sharp as stones stinging soles
        oyster shells slicing skin

I walk barefoot

                footpaths caving in
                bitumen crack/ing

a small breeze lifts leaves off the umbrella trees

            – there are tunnels
            like arteries
              under these streets
                from coal mines,
                  and World War II –

visible veins of subsidence

hard ground gives way to sand now
soft between toes
then gritty like granulated sugar
on the water's edge
I sit on the steps and count the coal ships
wonder what is out there

what my ancestors faced
as they crossed
the sea of atrocities
from Africa to Jamaica

or my great-grandfather's
mother tongue, Cymraeg,
suppressed by Y Deddfau Uno

seagulls loll in a puddle of sea
on the kids' pool
where Dad would canoe as a boy
a map carved out of concrete
the whole world beneath him

Snowdonia National Park

We passed bumblebees hovering clumsily near hedges
the intense green of sheep-filled pastures
crossed narrow stone bridges low over rapids
to reach the mountains streaked with lilac flowers
we climbed slippery grey shale
the stone pathway steep to the sky
a moment when I couldn't go any further
afraid to keep climbing
you scrambled higher and higher
to see how high you could go
even though you are the one scared of heights
from our separate spots we watched
people below stopping their cars at the edge of the lake
to stretch and breathe the summer air
then the Hawks came
around the side of the mountain
so close their sonic boom
almost knocked us off our feet
they passed us in a moment
swooping across the lake
disappearing silence

Drought

Today the rain came
but it was 'fake rain'
not enough water to drench this
dry island.
'The world is off its axis,
since the earthquake in Haiti,
and only Mother Nature can fix it,'
the taxi driver said.
Bleached-bone clouds
sock the mountains
but they won't bring rain
just mist as thick as smoke
obscuring the view of Kingston.
We hope real rain soon comes
rain that fills drains
and slicks cotton to skin.
Not flooding rain or hurricane
but real rain
real rain

Long Mountain House (College Common)

Facing towards the spill of houses
of Newcastle
and the mansions of Jacks Hill
on the edge
of the Blue Mountains
in shades of red
the afternoon breeze
has come rattling the heavy canopy
hanging over the external staircase
easing the humidity.
I'm told my grandma
was born near here
and I feel closer to her now
but not totally
my self still in
Louisiana, New York,
Miami

some things are familiar,
as Juliet said they would be—
names like Newcastle and the Blue Mountains,
the fuchsia bougainvillea Mum loves so much
spilling wildly over fences,
weatherboard houses, and grassy, guttered footpaths—
but nothing else is the same

there is blood on my hands
cut by the metal latch
of the ATM security door
and the cuts circling
my ankle
from tripping over a thorny branch
on the overgrown footpath

my blood
dripping
to the ground

Drifting

My diary entries end at:
'Thursday
tanks entered Denham Town.'
On Monday the 6pm curfew had been called;
the next day
I walked along the grassy footpath
of the University of the West Indies campus
the heat cocooning me,
causing mirages of people walking
in the distance.

The campus was empty,
only security gathered in groups
where the roads met
or cruised past in cars.

Clouds hovered
amidst the peaks
of the Blue Mountains
always promising rain,
but no rain came.

At the library
whispered conversations
'but they are innocent people,'
'then they should leave.'

The ground swallowed me then
the air like a wet towel smothering me
as I walked the long walk home
to the sound of nothing.

Metamorphosis

Swarms of yellow
in the morning
when the light still
streaks white
they dot the trees
and are all I can see in
the spaces.
A butterfly
is an exhalation of breath
carrying the name of the deceased
their soul inhabiting *this place*
for a period so brief
but what is time
in a swarm of yellow butterflies?
Names are inscribed
in the tissue of wings—
Dorrit
Beulah
Elvira
Billy
Vivia
Augustus
Doris…
my ancestors'
souls released
from their chrysalis
an abundant mass
the colour of little suns

Dermis

your skin
layered sweet, layered thick
with ointment made from
soft orange flesh,
sweet
soft stink of Pawpaw
shield
on lips, on hands, on fingertips

your skin was powder,
baby down feathers in morning breeze
I would touch your earlobes, your arms,
the flexion creases of your daily routine

and your thick black hair
you plaited and spun with fingertips
kinks of paths of here and there
from end to root

    ovals in cross-section

but my hair grew blonde
honey-hued like the darkened comb
skin the shade of olive oil
you coated in Calamine
to ease the sting
painted cool dusty white, uneven
over mozzie bites, and scabs,
and here below the eye
one scar
remains

she is there

near as a mirage is near
present, as a ghost is present
her voice
lilts and sways, laces
between words,
between the phrase and
Jack and Jill went up the hill
to fetch a pail of…
the flutter of moth wings
flitting
between light and shadow
nectar and sky
her voice
resounding there
between words
forgotten
by her Grandchild
reciting
English nursery rhymes

Stockton

From The Hill,
across the water,
past the turret of Jesmond House
and the servants' quarters I lived in surreptitiously,
are the sand dunes rolling softly out to sea.
For over thirty years the dunes have been mined
for rutile, zircon, ilmenite and silica

I remember a story of a horse rider plunging into sand

        trapped   sunken

if you walk along the dunes
from Stockton Bight towards the city
you come to the town, and the beach,
her body sinking supine
with the smells of Bloodwood and Blackbutt
a digit, a tibia wedged into sand
like the Sygna shipwrecked off the coast
the year I was born.

Here the salt is thick,
not sulphuric like the canopy that covered the city,
this was Pirate Point where
convicts burned middens to make lime
their skin singeing in glaring sun
and the sky a washed-out hue of blue
they could barely see
where the horizon met or
ocean led into land.

Once, amongst the dunes I saw a man,
he used driftwood to keep him steady
we walked together for a long time
our feet diving in sand as we
trekked towards the sea, up and over
and down to cool gullies where

sometimes water forms lakes

but the sand had blown across the dunes
changing tracks of footprints
and when I looked back
all that was left were
motorbike marks and glints of
broken glass smooth
like riverstone

there are many atrocities here
that twilight obscures
like Wolff's law
the layering of bone upon bone

Eulogy

Before the bush began,
where I'd hide under leaves,
between trees, on damp soil,
was your world
the garage where we
rummaged through old things—
picks and hoes and rusty machines
and the garden
where you'd always be,
growing sweet peas
that twisted and climbed and
sprang back
like curls
and when she went
we listened while you sang
and hummed and sang again
Come! Come! Come to me, Thora,
Come once again and be
then comforted you
as you wept
for she was no longer here

Wayfinding

Was it a vision, or a waking dream?
      Fled is that music:—Do I wake or sleep?
          – John Keats, 'Ode to a Nightingale'

Mudlarks make bowl-like nests
blue wrens bounce from tree to tree
red wattlebirds show off their yellow chests
suspended upside down from the maple tree

Mum watched the birds
her hands as soft as down
knew their sacredness reified beyond words
observed the consequence of their sound

birdsong resonant in the in-between
wayfinding home, summoning sleep

Oval

On the flat
—where rain lay like drowned kittens' whey—
wind whipped dirt and rubbish
from cracks in soil lacteal

She bore three sons here…

the oval is bare
its edges squashed square
Stringybark and Iron Bark grew here
chickens and orchard fruits, then milk and cheese

a mesh of Kochia and Lantana chipped with hoes under a searing heat

—Dad saw a chicken run five times around him before it dropped
as if it still felt fear even though its head was on the block—

fear in bones
snap—
make a wish

milk soaks grass frost-white

and your hands were worn like riverbeds
seamed with silt
knuckles hard like pebbles
lodged in skin

inside, for the men
Grandma baked pumpkin scones, pot-roasted lamb and sea-salt
baked potatoes

Years on,
every Sunday
when we were kids
we'd run
up the driveway
for a taste
of that sweet salted meat

run up the driveway steep
to your house with the view of ships and the Obelisk
built on the hill
swapped by the Council
so they could make an oval on the flat
where rain lay like drowned kittens' whey
and teenagers smoke behind the brick toilet block.

Homes for Leaf-Curling Spiders

Leaves curled into shell,
only thin legs visible,
suspended from the lavender bush
like a garland of precious charms
each leaf distinct – crisp brown, sage green
entangled in a lace of silver

or is it a snail shell hung from the sky
a tiny planet, the moon
spider a hermit crab
in the centre of a spiral galaxy
surrounded by a halo of stars?

a history of nature and buildings

The line I trace with my feet
Walking to the museum
Is more important and more
Beautiful than the lines
I find there hung up
On the walls.   (Hundertwasser, Paris, 1953)

Through a slit narrow window
in the library wall,
Nature exists in an
organic state of chaos
far from the protective shell
of solid brick walls and
unbroken silence.
Inside are books stacked on shelves,
on desks, on return trolleys.
Books depicting topographic maps,
Bioregional histories and
Anarcho-syndicalist philosophies.
They have folded paper edges of
thumbed origami, and sticky-taped spines.
Maybe I will use the pages from these books,
fold them delicately,
and fly out the window in my paper aeroplane.

brisk

two white cranes with pencil-thin necks, flap their gracious wings against blue

mist rises from the creek as though it is scalding

brisk, is how you would describe this cold, cold morning where breath fogs in front of us like small puffs of smoke from early morning cigarettes

the creek is gentle today, as though there are more important things to do than rush

ducks sleep in the rushes, their heads buried so deep in feathers it's as if they have no heads at all

Heliotropism

Search for light
in leaden amber cool
the sun a nexus
for plants, animals,
all earthlife. Sunflecks —
a sharp intake of breath

sea urchin

baby sea urchins land on rocks / the way astronauts land on planets / hurtle through ocean space / in translucent eggs / the shape of moon landers / enter the turbulence of waves / eject into salt and spray / to live out the rest of their days / on the ocean floor / for fifty years / maybe more

on the beach / I found a dry sea urchin / pale indigo of waning summer sun / small as a fairy egg / it fit between / forefinger and thumb / tiny spiny orb / contoured by deep purple canyons /metamorphosing once again / emersion, from sea to air /a planet no longer in motion

Christmas Day (Sunset)

Stillness
as though lethargy has consumed the earth
and worms and Christmas beetles are hibernating
we look towards the coral-coloured sea
and the candy pink harbour
home to pods of charcoal dolphins
playing close to shore.
But what it is more unreal
more difficult to grasp
is that the lack of breeze on our skin
is not really stillness at all
but atoms and molecules
constantly fidgeting

Ma in the Moon

The silver-white boardwalk
edging the shoreline
is an illusion

I travel across the sky
the Big Dipper and
Saucepan my maps
a choreography of stars and planets
leading me to what appears in the gaps
on the moon's surface

a face shaped by shadows
serene as an egg
suspended in blue-black

if you stare long enough
the space
becomes all there is

connecting dazzling
balls of light
the size of pin-heads
the size of moons

New Year's Eve 2009

The water rests on
a seaweed nest
of autumnal browns
like leaves after rain
still now
shapeshifting from grey to blue

at the bottom of this lake
a razor fish is wearing my friend's glasses
knocked off the top of his head
while dragging his kayak back to shore
blindly he searched for them
it was New Year's Eve and fireworks
exploded in puffs of magic dust
–blue, orange, silver–
the sound like crackling kindling
around the lake's circumference
and in those twenty-four hours
it changed from the lake of my childhood
to a lake of possibility
as I waded tiptoe across slicing shells
before letting my body drop
into its depths

William and Tom

The sea cupped their boat in its palm placing them here on this continent where sandstone cliffs resemble faces of grief-stricken men.

They were friends, William and Tom, but they saw different paths in the lines marking their palms.

After many rainfalls, and many droughts, they were to meet again, forever friends

as though they had merely witnessed the stillness of a hair slowly drifting or a bird bracing to land

Home

If only this genealogical path
were simply
an ancestral desire line
rather than concentric circles
of unknowing

Bones

Dad's jacket is the colour of bone
it sits folded in the bottom drawer
of my cupboard
sporting leatherette shoulders and elbows.
Dad's bones creaked
like old furniture
ached when a storm was brewing.
               – Bones
crosshatched like kindling
–story, history, memory–
the scaffold of who we are

leafless branches swinging as though breaking

— for L M

At The Convent
you played me Emahoy Tsegué-Maryam Guèbrou
for the first time,
her music welcoming me like the tide

I'd bought Bella Li's *Argosy*
and we discussed how I really couldn't believe
that I hadn't read her poetry

and how I hadn't written anything
since Dad died, not really

you told me Emahoy had been a nun
and here we were within this old convent's
green speckled walls
our conversation a cartography

(later, in the cafe I read that Emahoy
had once sung for Haile Selassie)

we didn't speak of who lived here once
labelled 'wayward girls',
spectres in the windows

we didn't speak of religion
or transportation or loss

we both knew
why I had come

Notes

Poems in this collection have appeared, some in different form, in *Australian Poetry Anthology, Cordite Poetry Review, Rabbit, South Broadway Ghost Society, EnterText, Mod_Piece, Moko Magazine, Mother Nature Burns, antiTHESIS, Hecate, SWAMP, Interviewing the Caribbean, Flightpath, Violet, sx Salon, Nine Muses Poetry, small poems like bird feet, Invisible City* and *Mining*.

Italics in 'Cloudburst' quote the song 'It's Been Raining' by Kimya Dawson. *Hidden Vagenda*. 2004.

The textual source in '*calidris ruficollis* (smallest shorebird in Australia), a migration' is based on language in 'Red-necked Stint'. *BirdLife Australia*. 2012.
http://www.birdlife.org.au/bird-profile/red-necked-stint

Some language in 'White Spill' is borrowed, in different form, from the newspaper article 'Polystyrene "white spill" from Brisbane floods causing "environmental catastrophe" on Queensland beaches.' Tessa Mapstone, Sarah Howells, and Jacqui Street. *ABC Sunshine Coast*. Posted Thursday 10 March 2022.

Italics in 'Belgrave Rd' quote T. S. Eliot's 'The Waste Land.' *The Annotated Waste Land with Eliot's Contemporary Prose*. Ed and Intro. Laurence Rainey. New Haven: Yale University Press, 2005. 62-65.

Italics in 'Eulogy' quote the song 'Thora' by Fred E. Weatherly and Stephen Adams. London: Boosey & Co. 1905.

The lines *Was it a vision, or a waking dream? / Fled is that music:—Do I wake or sleep?* in 'Wayfinding' are taken from John Keats, 'Ode to a Nightingale'. *The Norton Anthology of Poetry*. Third Edition. Eds. Alexander W. Allison, Herbert Barrows et al. New York and London: W. W. Norton & Company, 1983. 660-662.

Italics in 'a history of nature and buildings' quotes Hundertwasser, Friedensreich, Joram Harel and Wieland Schmied. *Hundertwasser: KunstHausWien.* Köln: Taschen. 1999.

Acknowledgements

My gratitude to Ralph Wessman and Walleah Press for publishing this collection of poetry. Thank you so much to Kyoko Imazu for permission to use her beautiful artwork *Spiderweb* on the cover. Thank you to my friend Josie Newton for taking the author photograph. Sincere gratitude to Opal Palmer Adisa, A. Frances Johnson, and Shari Lynelle. Thank you to the Dr Writers group– Suzanne Hermanoczki, Shari Lynelle, Susan Pyke and Linda Weste–for their camaraderie and their invaluable feedback on my poems over the years. Thank you to Tony Birch and Marion M Campbell for their feedback and guidance. I was inspired by some of the wonderful poets I met at the Association of Caribbean Women Writers and Scholars Conference, Louisiana State University, Baton Rouge, Louisiana in 2010 and I thank them for their encouragement and generosity. Thank you to all the publications that have included my poetry in their pages. My heartfelt thanks to all my dear family and friends who have supported me through the writing of these poems. Thank you to Elnaz Nourizadeh for our wonderful chats and Leah Muddle for her kindness. Special thanks to my sister Karina for her support, adventures and invaluable advice. And thank you to Christine Mason for her continued encouragement and support. My deepest thanks to my partner Tom, and my children Freddy and River– every day is an adventure, and every tiny slater or hot air balloon floating by is a poem in waiting. To Ned and Mor Mor who lived life to the fullest, with gratitude, we miss you dearly. And to Seva, a lover of ideas. This book is dedicated with love to my wonderful Mum and Dad who are no longer with us but who are with me every day. They instilled in me my love of poetry, story and history and supported me unconditionally. And to my Ancestors.

www.ingramcontent.com/pod-product-compliance
Lightning Source LLC
Chambersburg PA
CBHW020548080526
44583CB00013B/1054